PUTTING THE PLANET FIRST

MAKING OUR FOOD SUSTAINABLE

PAUL MASON

CRABTREE
PUBLISHING COMPANY
WWW.CRABTREEBOOKS.COM

CRABTREE
PUBLISHING COMPANY
WWW.CRABTREEBOOKS.COM

Published in Canada
Crabtree Publishing
616 Welland Avenue
St. Catharines, ON
L2M 5V6

Published in the United States
Crabtree Publishing
PMB 59051
350 Fifth Ave, 59th Floor
New York, NY 10118

Published in 2019 by Crabtree Publishing Company

First Published in Great Britain in 2017 by Wayland
Copyright © Hodder and Stoughton, 2017

Printed in the U.S.A./082018/CG20180601

Author: Paul Mason

Editorial director: Kathy Middleton

Editors: Paul Mason, Elizabeth Brent, Ellen Rodger

Proofreader: Lorna Notsch

Interior design: Peter Clayman

Prepress technician: Ken Wright

Print coordinator: Katherine Berti

Images:
All images courtesy of Shutterstock except p6: Shutterstock/Ultrakwang; p7: wikimedia/Leslie Staton; p11: Getty Images/Huw Jones; p19: Getty Images/Frederic Courbet; p20: AJP/Shutterstock.com; p21: tusharkoley/Shutterstock.com; p25: subtik/iStock by Getty Images; p27: Getty Images/NurPhoto/Contributor. Grateful thanks to Barcombe Nursery and The Ethicurean for permission to reproduce the images on pages 11 and 15 respectively

Every attempt has been made to clear copyright. Should there be any inadvertent omission, please apply to the publisher for rectification.

The website addresses (URLs) included in this book were valid at the time of going to press. However, it is possible that contents or addresses may have changed since the publication of this book. No responsibility for any such changes can be accepted by either the author or the Publisher.

Library and Archives Canada Cataloguing in Publication

Mason, Paul, 1967-, author
        Making our food sustainable / Paul Mason.

(Putting the planet first)
Includes index.
Issued in print and electronic formats.
ISBN 978-0-7787-5030-7 (hardcover).--
ISBN 978-0-7787-5034-5 (softcover).--
ISBN 978-1-4271-2143-1 (HTML)

        1. Sustainable agriculture--Juvenile literature. 2. Food supply--Juvenile literature. 3. Food--Environmental aspects--Juvenile literature. I. Title.

S494.5.S86M33 2018   j630   C2018-902461-5
                                                              C2018-902462-3

Library of Congress Cataloging-in-Publication Data

Names: Mason, Paul, 1967- author.
Title: Making our food sustainable / Paul Mason.
Description: New York : Crabtree Publishing Company, [2019] |
   Series: Putting the planet first | Includes index.
Identifiers: LCCN 2018021420 (print) | LCCN 2018026366 (ebook) |
   ISBN 9781427121431 (Electronic) |
   ISBN 9780778750307 (hardcover) |
   ISBN 9780778750345 (pbk.)
Subjects: LCSH: Food industry and trade--Environmental aspects--Juvenile
   literature. | Sustainable agriculture--Juvenile literature. |
   Food-supply--Environmental aspects--Juvenile literature.
Classification: LCC TD195.F57 (ebook) | LCC TD195.F57 M373 2019 (print) |
   DDC 338.1--dc23
LC record available at https://lccn.loc.gov/2018021420

CONTENTS

WHAT IS SUSTAINABLE FOOD?

Sustainable **food causes as little harm to the environment as possible. It is grown with the future of the planet in mind.**

Here is just one example of non-sustainable versus sustainable food (there are many others later in this book):

CASE 1

A farmer adds lots of **chemicals** to the soil to make the plants grow better. The trouble is, the chemicals also drain the soil of **nutrients**. Next year, the farmer will have to add more chemicals. Eventually, even with chemicals added it will be difficult to grow food on the soil.

THIS IS NOT SUSTAINABLE!

CASE 2

The farmer decides not to use chemicals. Instead, the fields are used to grow several different crops. Each crop needs slightly different nutrients, so the soil is not drained. The farmer grows slightly less than with chemicals. But the soil is healthier for growing crops.

THIS IS SUSTAINABLE!

Crops being sprayed with insect-killing chemicals

WHY DO WE NEED SUSTAINABLE FOOD?

One big reason we need sustainable food is that the world's population is increasing every year:

IMAGINE THE WORLD IS A BUS

In 1900, there were **1.6 billion** passengers.

By 2000, there were **6 billion** passengers.

In 2050, experts think there will be **9.5 billion** passengers.

At the moment, we grow enough food to feed everyone. But as the population increases, we will need more food. It is unfair to feed ourselves now in a way that will make growing food harder in the future. That would mean future generations may not have enough to eat.

FAIR TRADE

Producers **are not always able to get a fair price for what they make and grow.** Fair trade **means they are paid fairly and can enjoy better working conditions.**

WHY IS FAIR TRADE IMPORTANT?

Consumers, or shoppers, pay a little more for a fair trade product. But it means producers make a fair wage and have a reliable market for their products.

When producers make a little more, they can afford to put money into improving their farms or communities. They build schools, clinics, or hospitals. Producers also invest more time and money in environmentally sound practices such as organic farming. This makes fair trade sustainable.

THE DEAL ON CANE SUGAR

Eighty percent of the world's sugar comes from sugar cane. The market sets the price. Small sugar cane farmers find it hard to make a living. Fair trade sets a minimum price that ensures them of a living.

Less than 1 percent of the world's sugar cane is fairtrade produced.

Global export trade in sugar is $42 billion dollars

Wild Rice has a bold, dark color and a long, slender shape

WILD RICE

Wild rice is a type of grass that grows in lakes and rivers in some areas of North America. **Indigenous** peoples have harvested wide rice for centuries.

Traditionally, wild rice was harvested by knocking the long grass with poles and collecting it in canoes. That is how the White Earth Band of Ojibwe still harvest rice in northwestern Minnesota.

The White Earth Band hand harvests in canoes without motors to ensure only ripe kernels are taken. Unripe kernels are left to mature and fall back into the water to reseed. This ensures a crop will grow next year. The Band sells its sustainable wild rice online and through stores that sell fair trade products. It puts the money back into **land recovery projects**, language programs, and sustainable energy.

WHERE IS YOUR FOOD FROM?

Food that comes from far away is usually less sustainable than food from nearby.

Trucks, ships, and planes are all used to transport food. They all release a gas called carbon dioxide, or CO_2. This gas is one of the causes of **global warming**. In some areas of the world, global warming has resulted in more **droughts** and desertification. Desertification means **fertile** land turns into desert unsuitable for growing food.

One feature of sustainable food is that it is grown nearby and not transported long distances. When food is transported shorter distances, less CO_2 is released.

WHERE IS YOUR LETTUCE FROM?

Driving lettuce from Morocco in Africa to London, England releases **754 pounds (342 kg) of CO_2**

Driving lettuce from Spain to London releases **408 pounds (185 kg) of CO_2**

Driving lettuce from Canterbury, England to London releases **24 pounds (10.7 kg) of CO_2**

Lettuce driven to market from a farm far away causes more pollution than buying lettuce from nearby.*

*These figures are based on truck journeys.

The Greenmarket Farmers' Market in Union Square, New York, is open four days a week.

GREENMARKET FARMERS' MARKETS

Greenmarket Farmers' Markets started in Union Square, New York City, in 1976. A few farmers from close to the city set up a market. It was a way for them to sell their crops directly to shoppers. It also gave New Yorkers a chance to buy fresh, locally grown food.

The idea of a farmers' market became so popular that today there are more than 50 similar markets in the area. Everything has to be grown in the region, rather than being transported a long distance. All the food also has to be grown or made by the people selling it. This means transporting the food to market has a smaller environmental impact.

HOW DOES YOUR FOOD REACH YOU?

Imagine your next meal being flown to your house in a helicopter. Sounds fun! But helicopters release a lot of pollution. This is not good if you want sustainable food.

Now imagine your next meal arriving at your house by bicycle. Bikes create ZERO pollution. In the sustainable-food game, the meal that arrives by bike is the winner.

TYPICAL FOOD TRANSPORT

Of course, food is not usually delivered by helicopter or bike. So how does it travel?

- Small trucks bring all kinds of food short distances
- Big trucks transport food thousands of miles or km
- Ships and trains are used for longer distances, especially for food that does not **spoil** quickly
- Airplanes carry fresh food long distances

Transporting food by air produces a LOT of pollution.

POLLUTION FROM FOOD TRANSPORT

1.61 pounds (0.733 kg) of CO_2 per 0.62 mile (1 km)

0.668 pounds (0.303 kg) of CO_2 per 0.62 miles (1 km)

0.236 pounds (0.107 kg) of CO_2 per 0.62 miles (1 km)

A Barcombe vegetable delivery box, ready to be left on a customer's doorstep.

FOOD-BOX DELIVERY PROGRAM

Every week in Barcombe, England, boxes of fresh food are packed for delivery. Most of the food is grown by Barcombe Nurseries. Almost everything else is grown by other farmers very close by. A tiny amount comes from farther away.

Once a selection of food has been packed into boxes, Barcombe's van sets out on its delivery round. Each box is delivered to the customer's door. Instead of hundreds of people making trips to the supermarket to buy food, just one van drives around delivering a whole week's worth of food.

Food-box delivery programs like this are a great way of making food more sustainable.

GROWING FOOD

Before your food even starts its journey to your table, it has already caused a lot of pollution. In fact, growing food often produces MORE pollution than transporting it.

83 percent of _____ **emissions** come from growing food

17 percent come _____ from everything else (storage, transport, etc.)

HOW CAN GROWING FOOD CAUSE SO MANY EMISSIONS?

To understand this, think about tomatoes.

If you like tomatoes, you probably like eating them all year. But in northern Europe and North America, tomatoes don't grow all through the year. You have two choices:

Choice 1
Buy tomatoes that have been flown or driven from somewhere hot.

Choice 2
Buy tomatoes grown nearby in a heated greenhouse.

Imagine you are a tomato lover in Sweden. Which is the best choice?

LONG-HAUL VERSUS GREENHOUSE TOMATOES

From what you learned on pages 8–11, you would probably guess the greenhouse tomatoes grown right in Sweden would create less CO_2. Guess again:

FROM SWEDEN

FROM SPAIN

Transport:
10.5 ounces (300 g)
Production:
8.1 ounces (230 g)
Fertilizers:
7 ounces (200 g)

Transport:
2.39 ounces (68 g)
Production:
134 ounces (3,800 g)
Fertilizers:
1.65 ounces (47 g)

Units: grams of CO_2 per kg of tomatoes

Tomatoes trucked in from Spain would cause fewer total emissions—even though the CO_2 created by shipping them is more than four times as high. This is because greenhouses require a lot of energy to create heat to grow tomatoes.

Most of our energy comes from burning **fossil fuels**. Doing this releases CO_2 into the air. When you add these CO_2 emissions into the tomato total, it has a big effect.

SEASONAL FOOD

Experts agree that eating local, seasonal food is a good way to eat sustainably. But what is seasonal food?

Most foods grow naturally during a particular season. For example, in southern Canada and the northern United States, tomatoes grow in summer. In southern California, tomatoes can be grown outside all year.

People eat food grown locally when it is in season. When it is not in season, they ship in food grown elsewhere.

OUT-OF-SEASON CHOICES

California produces 95 percent of the tomatoes used in the USA for processing into ketchup and sauces, as well as one third of the fresh crop. If you live in Michigan or Canada and want to buy fresh local tomatoes in January, they have to be grown in heated greenhouses.

The other choice would be to have tomatoes flown or trucked to you from somewhere hot. Both choices require burning a lot of fossil fuels.

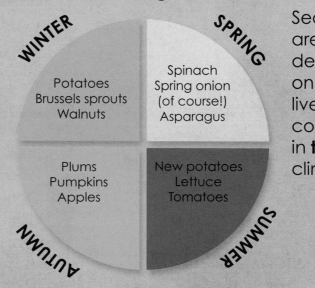

WINTER
Potatoes
Brussels sprouts
Walnuts

SPRING
Spinach
Spring onion
(of course!)
Asparagus

AUTUMN
Plums
Pumpkins
Apples

SUMMER
New potatoes
Lettuce
Tomatoes

Seasonal foods are different depending on where you live. These are common ones in **temperate** climates.

14

An Ethicurean chef picks part of the evening's menu.

THE ETHICUREAN

Near the English city of Bristol is a restaurant called The Ethicurean. Its mission is to show that seasonal food is more sustainable and more interesting than eating the same things all year.

The restaurant is next door to a walled garden, where a lot of its food is grown. This food really does not travel far before being eaten! The meat is either from local farms or hunted nearby.

Because what is growing outside changes all the time, the restaurant's menu also changes through the year.

PROTECTING THE SOIL

To be able to grow food in the future, we will need fertile **farmland. However, today's farming methods sometimes harm the land.**

INTENSIVE FARMING

Intensive farming is a way of getting a lot of crops from the land. There are big advantages to intensive farming. It is one of the ways we have been able to feed the world's increasing population. And getting more crops from the same amount of land has helped to keep food prices low.

However, intensive farming also causes problems. One of them is that the farms use chemical fertilizers to help the plants grow. If a lot of fertilizer is used, the soil can lose its natural nutrients, and become acidic. This makes it harder to grow crops.

THIS IS NOT SUSTAINABLE!

For example, in Japan, the use of chemical fertilizers grew 300 percent between 1950 and 1999.

1950
209 pounds
(95 kg)
per 2.5 acres
(1 ha)

1999
639 pounds
(290 kg)
per 2.5 acres
(1 ha)

This Japanese farmer grows her crops without using any chemicals.

BACK TO THE FUTURE

In some places, farmers are going back to techniques that were used before chemical fertilizers.

In Japan, almost all food is now grown using chemical fertilizers, but a small number of farmers will not use them. *Mukagaku hiyou* is the Japanese name for these crops, which means "grown without chemical fertilizers."

Some Japanese farmers are so determined not to harm the soil that they will not use ANY fertilizer. Even digging the soil or weeding is discouraged. This extreme form of sustainable farming is called *shizen noho*, which means "natural farming." *Shizen noho* crops are hard to find in stores, but when available, they are sold locally and in health-food stores.

BIODIVERSITY

Biodiversity is the range of different plants and animals that live in an area. It is important to sustainable farming.

WHY IS BIODIVERSITY NEEDED?

Two of the main reasons are:

1) Today's crops are descended from wild plants. If wild plants disappear, it will be harder to find new crops in the future.

2) Some wild plants survive drought and **pests** better than ordinary crops. Using these as farm crops is a way for farmers to adapt to changing conditions.

BIODIVERSITY AND INTENSIVE FARMING

Intensive farming (see page 16) may harm an area's biodiversity. On intensive farms, chemicals are used to kill other plants and insects that might damage the crop. The chemicals spread out and kill animals and plants nearby. This reduces biodiversity in the surrounding area.

At least 30,000 plants are edible

Humans only eat about 7,000 of them

There are 23,000 different plants around the world that could be used as food crops in the future.

Wild rooibos being picked in South Africa

WILD TEA

Rooibos tea comes from South Africa. It is popular around the world and is an important crop in its native country.

Rooibos only grows in a very small area of the country. Global warming is causing the climate there to get warmer and drier. The kind of rooibos farmers are currently growing may not be able to survive in the changing conditions.

Fortunately, a few people are still farming different kinds of wild rooibos. These are better at surviving in dry, hot conditions. In the future, these hardier types will mean the valuable rooibos tea industry can survive.

ORGANIC FOOD

People do not always mean the same thing when they talk about organic food. But organic food usually has most or all of the characteristics listed below.

WHAT MAKES FOOD ORGANIC?

Organic food is usually:
- grown in a way that does not harm the environment
- produced without using chemicals, such as artificial fertilizers and **pesticides**
- not kept unnaturally fresh, for example, by adding chemicals or other preservatives
- sold close to where it has been grown

All these are things that help make farming sustainable. Eating organic food is not the ONLY way to eat sustainable food, but it is one way.

An Indian farmer throws fertilizer over his crops. Using too much fertilizer can harm the soil.

Organic tea
being picked

THE SIKKIM ORGANIC MISSION

In 2003, the Indian state of Sikkim decided all its farms
would become completely organic.

Sikkim's landscapes range from giant
mountains to valleys with thick forests. There
are many different plants and rare animals. The
government wanted to protect this environment.
Artificial fertilizers and pesticides were banned. Village by village,
the government educated farmers about organic methods,
and it set up schools where people could study organic farming.

The **policy** has been a big success. Farmers are earning
more, because they do not have to buy chemical
fertilizers and pesticides. The natural landscape and
biodiversity have been preserved. The government even
says its people are happier as well.

MEAT AND VEGETABLES

A lot of people eat meat. Hamburgers might even be the world's most popular meal! Between 2010 and 2020, the amount of meat we eat is predicted to increase by 25 percent.

MEATY PROBLEMS

The trouble is, meat uses more land and **resources** than any other kind of food. Beef (for those popular burgers) is the worst offender.

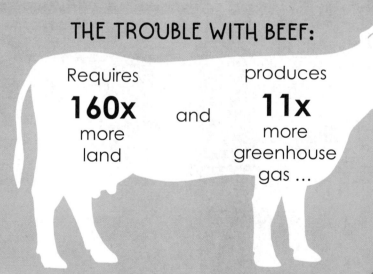

THE TROUBLE WITH BEEF:

Requires **160x** more land and produces **11x** more greenhouse gas ...

... COMPARED TO WHEAT OR RICE

COW GAS

Cattle are constantly expelling a gas called methane. Methane is one of the gases causing global warming. In fact, methane is 25 times as bad for the environment as CO_2.

Cow methane might not seem like a big problem until you realize there are almost a billion cows in the world. That's a lot of daily eruptions.

A tasty looking Veganuary
(or any time of year) pizza

VEGANUARY

Vegans are people who do not eat meat, fish, eggs, or dairy products such as milk and cheese. Because it does not include meat or dairy, vegan food is very sustainable.

In 2014, a group of vegans in the U.K. launched Veganuary. The name is a mash-up of vegan and January. The idea is that for the whole month of January, people try a vegan diet.

Veganuary is a way for people to eat less meat, and see whether they like a vegan diet. The Veganuary website has hundreds of recipes and suggestions for meat-free food, to help people throughout the month.

THE SLIPPERY PROBLEM OF FISH

For about half the world's population, fish has always been their main source of protein. Protein is necessary for the human body to grow and repair itself.

As the world's population grew in the 1900s, so did the amount of fish caught each year. By the 1950s, huge ships were being used to haul in millions of tons of fish every year.

This amount of fishing was unsustainable. The numbers of cod **plummeted**. There were not enough young to replace the grown fish that had been caught. This made it almost impossible for **stocks** of fish to increase again.

1645–1750
8.8 million tons (8 million metric tons) of cod is caught in 105 years

1953–1968
8.8 million tons (8 million metric tons) of cod is caught in 15 years

COD FISHING ON THE GRAND BANKS

By 1994, cod numbers on the Grand Banks, off the coast of Newfoundland, had fallen by 99 percent.

ICELANDIC COD

The Grand Banks are in the Atlantic Ocean southeast of Newfoundland. There is a similar cod-fishing area near Iceland. The story of Icelandic cod fishing is very different from the Grand Banks.

Iceland's government is determined that its cod will not be **overfished**. It sets limits on the number of fish that can be caught, and says that at least 20 percent of the cod caught must be at least four years old, based on its size.

This is because four years is the age at which cod start to reproduce. If there are not enough cod reproducing, the ones that are caught will not be replaced by new fish. If this happens, the government reduces the amount of cod that can be caught in the following year.

A large Icelandic cod being packed. Fish this size are regularly caught in Iceland, but have almost disappeared in other parts of the North Atlantic.

FOOD AND WATER

Global warming is making droughts in farming areas more common. This is a big problem, because everything we eat needs water to grow.

WATER-HUNGRY FOODS

Not all our food needs the same amount of water to grow. Some use a lot more than others. Producing 2.2 pounds (1 kg) of beef uses nearly 20 times as much water as producing the same weight of apples.

Water-hungry foods are not sustainable. They drain the surrounding area, making droughts worse. The next year, there is even less water available for growing food. Eventually, the local water supplies dry out.

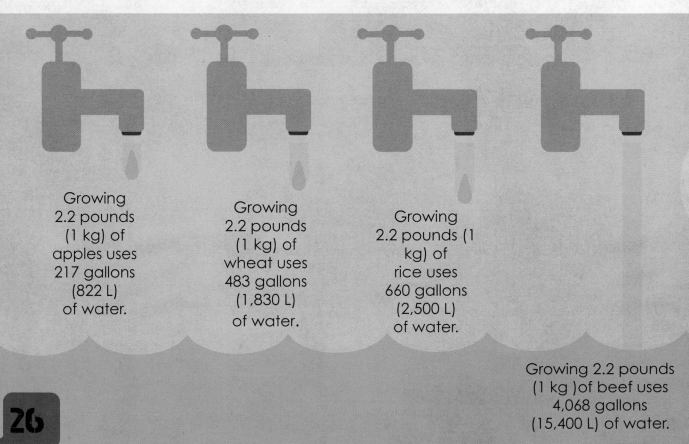

Growing 2.2 pounds (1 kg) of apples uses 217 gallons (822 L) of water.

Growing 2.2 pounds (1 kg) of wheat uses 483 gallons (1,830 L) of water.

Growing 2.2 pounds (1 kg) of rice uses 660 gallons (2,500 L) of water.

Growing 2.2 pounds (1 kg)of beef uses 4,068 gallons (15,400 L) of water.

Campaigners in Brazil tell people the watery cost of eating beef:

1 STEAK EQUALS 50 BATHS
PeTA

CUTTING YOUR VIRTUAL WATER

The water used to grow food is sometimes called virtual water. In Europe, each person consumes enough virtual water to fill an Olympic swimming pool every 18 months.

Fortunately, being careful what you eat can reduce the amount of virtual water you use. The Water Footprint Network (www.waterfootprint.org) can help. Its website has an interactive tool called Product Gallery. Clicking on a food tells you how much water is used to make 2.2 pounds (1 kg) of the food. For example:

• 2.2 pounds (1 kg) of sugar from sugar beets uses 243 gallons (920 L) of water, but from sugar cane it uses 471 gallons (1,782 L). It is more efficient to grow beets.

• 2.2 pounds (1 kg) of potatoes uses 73 gallons (287 L). The same weight of rice uses 659 gallons (2,497), or 10 times as much!

WASTED FOOD

Imagine you are really hungry. Someone puts your favorite pizza in front of you. Then they cut the pizza into thirds and take away one slice.

That slice represents how much of the world's food we waste every year.

ONE-THIRD WASTED

At least ONE-THIRD of the food we produce each year gets wasted. In poorer countries, food is often damaged during harvesting or spoils in storage after harvest. In wealthy countries, a lot of food is thrown away because it does not look perfect. Also, fresh food is bought, then stored for so long at home that it spoils and has to be thrown away.

Wasting less is one simple, easy way to supply more people with enough to eat. Immediately, the world's food would become more sustainable.

One year's global food waste

=

Five years' food grown in sub-Saharan Africa

Cassava being harvested in southern Africa

THE $1 MILLION CASSAVA PRIZE

Each year in Africa, enough food to feed 300 million people is wasted.

One of the **staple** foods in Africa is the cassava plant. Cassava grows underground, where it can last for a year or more and is able to survive droughts. But once cassava has been dug up, it starts to spoil within 15 minutes. A day or two later, it has to be thrown away.

A charity called Yieldwise thinks the world's scientists can solve this problem. It has offered a prize of $1 million (U.S.) to anyone who can come up with a way of keeping cassava fresh for longer.

GLOSSARY

chemical A liquid, solid, or gas

drought A long time without rain, which leads to a shortage of water

emission Something released into the air, usually a polluting gas

fair trade The practice of paying producers a fair price for their work and products

fertile Able to grow a lot of plants

fertilizer Material added to soil to make plants grow better

fossil fuels Coal, oil, and natural gas, which are all fuels made from the ancient remains of plants and animals

global warming Increase in the Earth's average temperature

Indigenous The original inhabitants

land recovery projects Recovering or regaining lands that once belonged to Indigenous peoples

nutrient Something that helps living things to grow and stay healthy

overfish To reduce the number of fish disastrously by catching too many

pest An insect or other animal that attacks crops

pesticide A chemical used to kill insects that could damage crops

plummet To go down very quickly

policy A course of action pursued by government or business

producers People who make, harvest, or grow things

resources Supplies of useful things, such as water or land

spoil To go rotten

staple Something used or needed regularly

stocks Reserves or stores of something

sustainable Something that can be maintained or kept going without doing harm

temperate Not hot and not extremely cold; temperate climates are usually warm and sometimes damp.

FINDING OUT MORE

WEBSITES

The Soil Association is a charity that sets rules about organic farming: www.soilassociation.org

Evergreen teaches about sustainability and cities. Its website includes information on school projects and videoes: www.evergreen.ca

The Center for Ecoliteracy's website has information on food and sustainability, ecological education, and interactive guides: www.ecoliteracy.org

FURTHER READING

Putting Your Carbon Foot In It: All About Environmental Meltdown and What You Can Do About It by Paul Mason (Wayland, 2012).

Food: From Field to Plate by Michael Bright (Crabtree, 2017).

Designing Green Communities by Janice Dyer (Crabtree, 2018).

INDEX